The Holy See's Teaching
on Catholic Schools

by

Archbishop J. Michael Miller

Solidarity Association
Atlanta, Georgia

Published for
Solidarity Association
245 Perimeter Center Parkway, Suite 610
Atlanta, GA 30346

by
Sophia Institute Press®
Box 5284, Manchester, NH 03108
1-800-888-9344
www.sophiainstitute.com

To order more copies,
contact Sophia Institute Press.

Library of Congress
Cataloging-in-Publication Data
Miller, J. Michael.
    The Holy See's teaching on Catholic
schools / by J. Michael Miller.
        p. cm.
    Includes bibliographical references.
    ISBN-13: 978-1-933184-20-3
(pbk. : alk. paper)
        1. Catholic schools — United States.
2. Education — Papal documents. I. Title.
    LC501.M477 2006
    371.071′273 — dc22   2006006326

Contents

iii

Introduction

On September 15, 2005, the Solidarity Association sponsored a conference in Washington that brought together leaders with a passionate interest in the future of Catholic education in our nation. After intense discussion, they concluded that, forty years after the promulgation of the Second Vatican Ecumenical Council's Declaration on Christian Education, *Gravissimum Educationis*, the signs of the times require that new wine be poured into the wineskins of America's Catholic schools. Affirming the June 2005 statement of the American bishops, *Renewing Our Commitment to Catholic Elementary and Secondary Schools in the Third Millennium*, the participants committed themselves to ensuring that "truly Catholic" elementary and secondary schools be "available, accessible, and affordable, to all Catholic parents and their children."[1]

The meeting acknowledged the irreplaceable role that Catholic schools play in the new evangelization of America and sought to foster the cooperation of all those involved in this apostolic work. The duty of educating the young is an ecclesial responsibility shared by all members of the Body of Christ: bishops, teachers, parents, and concerned lay leaders.

By her very nature, the Church has the right and the obligation to proclaim the Gospel to all nations (cf. Matt. 28:20). In the words of Vatican II's *Gravissimum Educationis*:

> To fulfill the mandate she has received from her divine founder of proclaiming the mystery of salvation to all men and of restoring all things in Christ, Holy Mother the Church must be concerned with the whole of man's

life, even the secular part of it, insofar as it has a bearing on his heavenly calling. Therefore, she has a role in the progress and development of education.[2]

Catholic schools participate in the Church's evangelizing mission of bringing the gospel to the ends of the earth. Particularly, they are places for the evangelization of the young. As ecclesial institutions, they are "the privileged environment in which Christian education is carried out."[3] Like Catholic colleges and universities, Catholic schools proceed *ex corde Ecclesiae*, from the very heart of the Church. America's Catholic schools, if they are to be genuinely Catholic, must be integrated into the organic pastoral program of the parish, the diocese, and the universal Church.[4]

From the days of their first appearance in the United States, Catholic schools have generously served the needs of the socially and economically disadvantaged. The parochial school system has integrated millions of young Catholics into ecclesial and social life. The Solidarity Association, whose name recalls the heritage of our beloved Pope John Paul II, follows in the long tradition of St. Angela Merici, St. Elizabeth Ann Seton, St. Marguerite Bourgeoys, St. Jean Baptiste de la Salle, St. John Bosco, and countless other religious and lay people who generously dedicated themselves to Christ's love for the poor, the disadvantaged, and the marginalized, as well as for the wealthy and for middle- and working-class Catholics.

This booklet, based on my intervention at the conference sponsored by the Solidarity Association, deals with the Holy See's teaching on Catholic education. Although this theme is far too vast to be adequately summarized in a few pages, I will introduce the major concerns found in post-conciliar Vatican publications on the subject. These include various papal interventions, the 1983 *Code of Canon*

Law in its section on schools, and the five major documents published by the Congregation for Catholic Education since Vatican II: *The Catholic School* (1977); *Lay Catholics in Schools: Witnesses to Faith* (1982); *The Religious Dimension of Education in a Catholic School* (1988); *The Catholic School on the Threshold of the Third Millennium* (1997); and *Consecrated Persons and Their Mission in Schools: Reflections and Guidelines* (2002). Among these documents, in particular I recommend for further study *The Catholic School* and *The Religious Dimension of Education in a Catholic School*.

After a preliminary statistical look at the current situation, I will discuss parental and government rights in education and the five benchmarks that can be used to judge a school's Catholic identity and thereby take the steps necessary to strengthen it.

I. The Current Situation of America's Catholic Schools

Certainly there is much to applaud in the American Catholic school system that currently enrolls almost 2.5 million students in its primary and secondary schools. By any measure this is an outstanding testimony to the vigor of Catholic life in the United States.

Even so, we cannot hide the fact that the number of students in Catholic schools continues to decline. The peak was reached in 1965 when 5.5 million students were enrolled in Catholic elementary and high schools. In 1930, there were more Catholic elementary schools (7,225), with 2.5 million students, than in 2004 (6,574), with

1.78 million students. Moreover, in the same seventy-five-year period, the Catholic population tripled: from 20.2 million in 1930 to over 66 million in 2004.

Since 1990, more than 400 new Catholic schools have opened in the United States. But during that period there has been a net loss of more than 760 Catholic schools. Most of the decline has been concentrated in urban, inner city, and rural areas.[5]

Clearly the Church in America is facing a serious challenge in serving her children and young people, one that cannot be swept under the rug or dismissed as the inevitable result of an increasingly secularized society.

FROM RELIGIOUS TO LAY LEADERSHIP

In the past forty years, not only in the United States but also in most of the developed world, religious vocations have plummeted. In 1965, there were 180,000 religious sisters in the United States; today there are fewer than 75,000, of whom more than 50 percent are over seventy years of age. Moreover, in 1965 there were 3.95 sisters for every 1,000 Catholics; in 2002, there was 1.16.[6]

Since Vatican II, Catholic elementary and secondary schools have shown a steady decline in the number of religious and priests who are administrators and teachers, and an increase in the number of laypersons who fill those positions.[7] Today religious women constitute less that 4 percent of the full-time professional staff of Catholic schools, while 95 percent of the teachers are laypersons.

For generations religious women provided the backbone of the parochial school system in the United States, contributing to its establishment and allowing it to flourish by their generous and sacrificial apostolate. In its documents, the Holy See frequently extols the specific contribution made by religious to the Church's educational apostolate:

Because of their special consecration, their particular experience of the gifts of the Spirit, their constant listening to the word of God, their practice of discernment, their rich heritage of pedagogical traditions built up since the establishment of their Institute, and their profound grasp of spiritual truth [cf. Eph. 2:17], consecrated persons are able to be especially effective in educational activities and to offer a specific contribution to the work of other educators.[8]

Undoubtedly, for years, the presence of religious in most parochial and secondary schools served as a built-in guarantee of their Catholic identity, which parents and pastors took for granted. And the vast network of schools established did indeed provide a sound religious and academic education, especially for Catholic immigrant children. The shift to lay leadership in Catholic schools, which has followed from the dearth of religious, presents its own set of challenges.

In no way do I wish to suggest that the laity are somehow second-best as Catholic educators. Still, theirs is a new responsibility and presents a new opportunity for the Church, one full of promise and hope. They, too, have a "supernatural vocation"[9] as educators.

To be effective bearers of the Church's educational tradition, however, laypersons who teach in Catholic schools need a "religious formation that is equal to their general, cultural, and, most especially, professional formation."[10] It is up to the ecclesial community to see to it that such formation is required of and made available to all Catholic-school educators, those already in the system and those preparing to enter it. In this regard, Catholic universities have a special responsibility to assist Catholic schools by providing teacher training courses and programs serving this constituency.

Some Catholic teachers bring to their educational apostolate the charism of a particular religious institute, with all that it involves in terms of a specific spirituality and approach to pedagogy. This is highly commendable. But more important than handing on elements of a particular charism to certain members of the laity is safeguarding and promoting schools' Catholic ethos. We cannot forget that a school is *first* Catholic before it can be molded according to the specific charism of a religious institute.

In light of the teaching of the Second Vatican Ecumenical Council that "lay people have their own proper competence in the building up of the Church,"[11] I believe that men and women, precisely as members of the lay faithful, have their own charism of teaching, independent of the charism of a particular religious congregation.

In the not-too-distant future, individual religious communities might die out or might flourish once again — we do not know. What we do know, however, is that the Church herself will survive; and she must have schools that are recognizably Catholic.

II. Shared Responsibilities

The Church's clear teaching, constantly reiterated by the Holy See, affirms that parents are the first educators of their children. Parents have the original, primary, and inalienable right to educate their offspring in conformity with the family's moral and religious convictions.[12] They are educators because they are parents. At the same time, the vast majority of parents share their educational responsibilities with other individuals and institutions, primarily the school.

Elementary education is, then, "an extension of parental education; it is extended and cooperative home schooling."[13] In a true sense schools are extensions of the home. Parents — and not schools

9

either of the state or the Church — have the primary moral responsibility of educating children to adulthood. Like a good Mother, the Church offers help to families by establishing Catholic schools that ensure the integral formation of their children.[14]

In keeping with a basic tenet of Catholic social doctrine, the principle of subsidiarity must always govern relations among families, the Church, and the state. As Pope John Paul II wrote in his 1994 *Letter to Families*:

> Subsidiarity thus complements paternal and maternal love and confirms its fundamental nature, inasmuch as all other participants in the process of education are only able to carry out their responsibilities in the name of the parents, with their consent, and, to a certain degree, with their authorization.[15]

For subsidiarity to be effective, families must enjoy true liberty in deciding how their children are to be educated. This means that "in principle, a state monopoly of education is not permissible, and that only a pluralism of school systems will respect the fundamental right and the freedom of individuals — although the exercise of this right may be conditioned by a multiplicity of factors, according to the social realities of each country."[16] Thus, the Catholic Church upholds "the principle of a plurality of school systems in order to safeguard her objectives."[17]

RIGHT TO GOVERNMENT
FINANCIAL ASSISTANCE

A pressing problem for Catholic schools in the United States is the lack of government financial assistance. The Church's teaching authority has frequently addressed the rights of parents to such help in fulfilling their obligation to educate their children. At Vatican II, the Fathers declared that "the public power, which has the obligation to protect and defend the rights of citizens, must see to it, in its concern for distributive justice, that public subsidies are paid out in such a way that parents are truly free to choose according to their conscience the schools they want for their children."[18]

The *Compendium of the Social Doctrine of the Church* (2005) states laconically that "the refusal to provide public economic support to non-public schools that need assistance and that render a service to civil society is to be considered an injustice."[19] Furthermore, the state is obliged to provide such public subsidies because of the enormous contribution that Catholic schools make to society by serving the common good.[20]

Most countries with substantial Christian majorities accept this obligation in justice: Australia, Belgium, Canada, England, France, Germany, Ireland, the Netherlands, Spain, and Scotland, to name a few. Their governments give Catholic schools financial assistance, some up to 100 percent. Italy,

Mexico, China, Cuba, North Korea, and the United States are exceptions in withholding assistance.

For many families, especially those in the working and middle classes, the financial burden of providing Catholic education for their children is sizeable and often too great. Since 1990, the average tuition in elementary and secondary Catholic schools has more than doubled. In 2004, it stood at $2,432 for elementary schools and $5,870 for secondary schools.

As the American bishops recently stated, there is no other way to address this question of cost than "to advocate for parental school choice and personal and corporate tax credits."[21] To advocate for some kind of government funding for Catholic education, as long as no unacceptable strings are attached, is the responsibility not just of parents of school-age children, but of all Catholics in their pursuit of justice. Too often Catholic Americans fail to appreciate that they have a *right* to subsidies for their schools because these institutions provide a service to society. In no way would such assistance compromise the constitutional separation of Church and state. Rather, it guarantees the fundamental right of parents to choose a school for their children.

Where the government bears its fair share of the financial burden, Catholic schools can flourish. Take the example of Melbourne, Australia. Melbourne is about the size of Houston; both cities have about four million inhabitants and more than one million Catholics. To serve its Catholic children, Melbourne has 256 elementary schools in its archdiocese and sixty-five secondary schools, compared with the Houston Archdiocese's fifty-two elementary and nine high schools. Why the difference? No doubt the answer lies in the generous public funding made available to Melbourne's Catholic schools.

Without some kind of government assistance or at least tax relief, it is difficult to see how Catholic education can remain affordable and accessible, especially to the increasing numbers of immigrant children, primarily Hispanics. Within less than a generation, Hispanics will constitute more than 50 percent of American Catholics and an even higher proportion of our Catholic children.

All Catholic children, not just those whose families have the financial means, have a right to a Catholic education. Vatican documents stress that the Church's preferential option for the poor means that she offers her educational ministry in the first place to "those who are poor in the goods of this world."[22] The Holy See supports the concern of the American bishops to provide for the poor and those who might be underprepared for high academic achievement: the Catholic school "is a school for all, with special attention to those who are weakest."[23] Guaranteeing this "for all" will require a new politics of educational funding in the United States.

III. Five Essential Marks of Catholic Schools

Papal interventions and Roman documents repeatedly emphasize that certain characteristics must be present for a school to be considered authentically Catholic. Like the marks of the Church proclaimed in the Creed — one, holy, catholic, and apostolic — so, too, does the Holy See identify the principal features of a school as *Catholic*: a Catholic school should be inspired by a supernatural vision, founded on Christian anthropology, animated by communion and community, imbued with a Catholic worldview throughout its curriculum, and sustained by gospel witness. These benchmarks help to answer the critical question: *Is this a Catholic school according to the mind of the Church?*

Pope John Paul II reminded a group of American bishops during their 2004 *ad limina* visit:

> It is of utmost importance, therefore, that the Church's institutions be genuinely Catholic: Catholic in their self-understanding and Catholic in their identity.[24]

It is precisely because of its Catholic identity, which is anything but sectarian, that a school derives the originality that enables it to be a genuine instrument of the Church's evangelizing mission.[25] Michael Guerra, former president of the National Catholic Educational Association put the challenge succinctly: "The first and most important task for Catholic schools is to maintain and continually strengthen their Catholic identity."[26]

The five elements that necessarily belong to a school's Catholic identity are the principles proposed by the Holy See that justify the Church's heavy investment in schooling. Moreover, they are measurable benchmarks, forming the backbone and inspiring the mission of every Catholic school.

Let us now look at each of the marks that give a school a Catholic identity.

1. INSPIRED BY A SUPERNATURAL VISION

The Church sees education as a process that, in light of man's transcendent destiny, forms the whole child and seeks to fix his or her eyes on heaven.[27] The specific purpose of a Catholic education is the formation of boys and girls who will be good citizens of this world, loving God and neighbor and enriching society with the leaven of the gospel, and who will also be citizens of the world to come, thus fulfilling their destiny to become saints.[28]

In a speech addressed to American Catholic educators in New Orleans, Pope John Paul II presented them with

> the pressing challenge of clearly identifying the aims of Catholic education, and applying proper methods in Catholic elementary and secondary education. . . . It is the challenge of fully understanding the educational enterprise, of properly evaluating its content,

and of transmitting the full truth concerning the human person, created in God's image and called to life in Christ through the Holy Spirit.[29]

An emphasis on the inalienable dignity of the human person — above all on his or her spiritual dimension — is especially necessary today. Unfortunately, far too many in government, business, the media, and even the educational establishment perceive education to be merely an instrument for the acquisition of information that will improve the chances of worldly success and a more comfortable standard of living. Such an impoverished vision of education is not Catholic.

If Catholic educators, parents, and others who dedicate themselves to this apostolate fail to keep in mind a high supernatural vision, all their talk about Catholic schools will be no more than "a gong booming or a cymbal clashing" (1 Cor. 13:1).

2. FOUNDED ON A
CHRISTIAN ANTHROPOLOGY

Emphasis on the supernatural destiny of students brings with it a profound appreciation of the need to perfect children in all their dimensions as images of God (cf. Gen. 1:26-27). Catholic theology teaches that grace builds on nature. Because of this complementarity of the natural and the supernatural, Catholic educators should have a sound understanding of the human person that addresses the requirements of both the natural and the supernatural perfection of the children entrusted to their care.[30]

Repeatedly the Holy See's documents emphasize the need for an educational philosophy built on a correct understanding of who the human person is. How do they describe such an anthropological vision?

In *Lay Catholics in Schools: Witnesses to Faith*, the Vatican proposes a response:

In today's pluralistic world, the Catholic educator must consciously inspire his or her activity with the Christian concept of the person, in communion with the Magisterium of the Church. It is a concept which includes a defense of human rights, but also attributes to the human person the dignity of a child of God. . . . It calls for the fullest development of all that is human, because we have been made masters of the world by its Creator. Finally, it proposes Christ, Incarnate Son of God and perfect Man, as both model and means; to imitate him is, for all men and women, the inexhaustible source of personal and communal perfection.[31]

All this says nothing more than the words from the Pastoral Constitution on the Church in the Modern World, so frequently quoted by Pope John Paul II: "It is only in the mystery of the Word made flesh that the mystery of man truly becomes clear."[32]

A Catholic school, therefore, cannot be a factory for the learning of various skills and competencies designed to fill the echelons of business and industry. Nor is it for "clients" and "consumers" in a competitive marketplace that values academic achievement. Education is not a commodity, even if Catholic schools equip their graduates with enviable skills. Rather, "the Catholic school sets out to be a school for the human person and of human persons."[33]

The Holy See's documents insist that, in order to be worthy of its name, a Catholic school must be founded on Jesus Christ, the Redeemer. It is he who, through his Incarnation, is united with each student. Christ is not an afterthought or an add-on to Catholic educational philosophy; he is the center and fulcrum of the entire enterprise, the light enlightening every boy and girl who comes into a

Catholic school (cf. John 1:9). In its document *The Catholic School*, the Sacred Congregation for Catholic Education states:

> The Catholic school is committed thus to the development of the whole man, since in Christ, the perfect man, all human values find their fulfillment and unity. Herein lies the specifically Catholic character of the school. Its duty to cultivate human values in their own legitimate right in accordance with its particular mission to serve all men has its origin in the figure of Christ. He is the one who ennobles man, gives meaning to human life, and is the model which the Catholic school offers to its pupils.[34]

The gospel of Jesus Christ and his very person are to inspire and guide the Catholic school in every dimension of its life and activity — its philosophy of education, its curriculum, its community life, its selection of teachers, and even its physical environment.

Christ is *the* Teacher in Catholic schools. Nevertheless, this conviction, in its very simplicity, can sometimes be overlooked. Catholic schools have the task of being the living and provocative memory of Christ. All too many Catholic schools fall into the trap of a secular academic success culture, putting their Christological focus and its accompanying understanding of the human person in second place. Christ is "fitted in" rather than being the school's vital principle.

As John Paul II wrote in his 1979 Message to the National Catholic Educational Association, "Catholic education is above all a question of communicating Christ, of helping to form Christ in the lives of others."[35] Authentic Catholic educators recognize Christ and his understanding of the human person as the measure of a school's catholicity. He is "the foundation of the whole educational enterprise in a Catholic school,"[36] and the principles of his gospel are its guiding educational norms:

> In a Catholic school, everyone should be aware of the living presence of Jesus the "Master" who, today as always, is with us in our journey through life as the one genuine "Teacher," the perfect Man in whom all human values find their fullest perfection. The inspiration of Jesus must be translated from the ideal into the real. The gospel spirit should be evident in a Christian way of thought and life which permeates all facets of the educational climate.[37]

3. ANIMATED BY COMMUNION
AND COMMUNITY

A third mark of catholicity is the emphasis on the school as a community — a community of persons and, even more to the point, "a genuine community of faith."[38] Such an emphasis proposes an alternative model for Catholic schools to that of an individualistic society. This communal dimension is rooted both in the social nature of the human person and in the reality of the Church as "the home and the school of communion."[39] That the Catholic school is an educational *community* "is one of the most enriching developments for the contemporary school."[40] The Congregation's *Religious Dimension of Education in a Catholic School* sums up this new emphasis:

The declaration *Gravissimum Educationis* notes an important advance in the way a Catholic school is thought of: the transition from the school as an institution to the school as a community. This community dimension is, perhaps, one result of the new awareness of the Church's nature as developed by the Council. In the Council texts, the community dimension is primarily a theological concept rather than a sociological category.[41]

The Holy See describes the school as a community in four areas: the teamwork among all those involved; the cooperation between educators and bishops; the interaction of students with teachers; and the school's physical environment.

Teamwork

Elementary schools "should try to create a community school climate that reproduces, as far as possible, the warm and intimate atmosphere of family life. Those responsible for these schools will, therefore, do everything they can to promote a common spirit of trust and spontaneity."[42] This means that educators should develop a willingness to collaborate among themselves. Teachers, both religious and lay, together with parents and school-board members, are to work as a team for the school's common good.[43] Their communion fosters appreciation of the various charisms and vocations that build up a genuine school community and strengthen scholastic solidarity.[44] Educators, administrators, parents, and bishops guide the school to make choices that promote "overcoming individualistic self-promotion, solidarity instead of competition, assisting the weak instead of marginalization, responsible participation instead of indifference."[45]

The Holy See is, moreover, ever mindful of ensuring the appropriate involvement of parents in Catholic schools:

> Close cooperation with the family is especially important when treating sensitive issues such

as religious, moral, or sexual education, orientation toward a profession, or a choice of one's vocation in life. It is not a question of convenience, but a partnership based on faith.[46]

Now, more than in the past, teachers and administrators must often encourage parental participation in the school's mission and life. Such a partnership is directed not just toward dealing with academic problems but also toward planning and evaluating the effectiveness of the school's mission.

Even though consecrated men and women are now few in the schools, the witness of their collaboration with the laity enriches the ecclesial value of educational communities. As "experts in communion" because of their experience in community life, religious foster those "human and spiritual bonds that promote the mutual exchange of gifts" with all others involved in the school.[47] In the words of a recent Vatican document:

> Consecrated persons are thus leaven that is able to create relations of increasingly deep communion that are themselves educational. They promote solidarity, mutual enhancement, and joint responsibility in the educational plan, and, above all, they give an explicit Christian testimony.[48]

Cooperation Between Educators and Bishops

The catholicity of American schools also depends largely on the bonds of ecclesial communion between bishops and Catholic educators. They are to help one another in carrying out the task to which they are mutually committed. Personal relationships marked by mutual trust, close cooperation, and continuing dialogue are required for a genuine spirit of communion.

First, trust. This goes beyond the personal relationships of those involved. These might or might not be marked by warmth and friendship, depending on the concrete situation. The more profound foundation for such trust is shared adherence to the person of Jesus Christ. Trust is fostered by listening to one another, by respecting the different gifts of each, and by recognizing one another's specific responsibilities. With trust comes dialogue. Both bishops and educators, whether singly or in associations, should avail themselves of open, sincere, and regular dialogue in their joint efforts on behalf of Catholic schools.

Educators and ecclesial authorities should cooperate closely in fostering a school's catholicity. Such collaboration is not only an ideal but also a time-honored ecclesial practice in the United States. A spirituality of communion should be the guiding principle of Catholic education. Without this spiritual path, all external structures of cooperation serve very little purpose; they would be mere mechanisms without a soul.[49]

Catholic educators recognize that the bishop's pastoral leadership is pivotal in supporting the establishment and ensuring the catholicity of the schools in his pastoral care. Indeed, "only the bishop can set the tone, ensure the priority, and effectively present the importance of the cause to the Catholic people."[50] His responsibility for Catholic schools derives from the *munus docendi*, the office of teaching, he received at ordination.[51] As the Code of Canon Law states, "Pastors of souls have the duty of making all possible arrangements so that all the faithful may avail themselves of a Catholic education."[52]

With regard to Catholic schools, episcopal responsibility is twofold. First, the bishop must integrate schools into his diocese's pastoral program; and, second, he must oversee the teaching within them. As John Paul II straightforwardly affirmed,

"Bishops need to support and enhance the work of Catholic schools."[53]

The bishop must see to it that the education in his schools is based on the principles of Catholic doctrine. This vigilance includes even schools established or directed by members of religious institutes.[54] The bishop's particular responsibilities include ensuring that teachers are sound in their doctrine and outstanding in their integrity of life.[55] It is he who must judge whether the children in the Catholic schools in his diocese are receiving the fullness of the Church's faith in their catechetical and religious formation.

It is important that the bishop be involved in Catholic schools not only by exercising veto power — whether over texts, curricula, or teachers — but also by taking an active role in fostering the specifically Catholic ethos of schools under his jurisdiction. In an *ad limina* address to a group of American bishops in June 2004, Pope John Paul II summed up this point: "The Church's presence in elementary and secondary education must . . . be the object of your special attention as shepherds of the People of God."[56] In particular, pastors should set in place "specific programs of formation" that will enable the laity to take on responsibilities for teaching in Catholic schools.[57]

Interaction of Students with Teachers

The Catholic philosophy of education has always paid special attention to the quality of interpersonal relations in the school community, especially those between teachers and students. This concern ensures that the student is seen as a person whose intellectual growth is harmonized with spiritual, religious, emotional, and social growth.[58] Because, as St. John Bosco said, "education is a thing of the heart,"[59] authentic formation of young people requires the personalized accompanying of a teacher. "During childhood and adolescence a student needs to experience personal relations with outstanding educators, and what is taught has greater influence on the student's formation when placed in a context of personal involvement, genuine reciprocity, coherence of attitudes, lifestyle, and day-to-day behavior."[60] Direct and personal contact between teachers and students is a hallmark of the Catholic school. A learning atmosphere that encourages the befriending of students is far removed from the caricature of the remote disciplinarian cherished by the media.

In measured terms, the Congregation's document *Lay Catholics in Schools: Witnesses to Faith* describes the student-teaching relationship:

> A personal relationship is always a dialogue rather than a monologue, and the teacher must be convinced that the enrichment in the relationship is mutual. But the mission must never be lost sight of: the educator can

never forget that students need a companion and guide during their period of growth; they need help from others in order to overcome doubts and disorientation. Also, rapport with the students ought to be a prudent combination of familiarity and distance; and this must be adapted to the need of each individual student. Familiarity will make a personal relationship easier, but a certain distance is also needed.[61]

Catholic schools, then, safeguard the priority of the person, both student and teacher. They foster the proper friendship between them, since "an authentic formative process can only be initiated through a personal relationship."[62]

Physical Environment

A school's physical environment is also an integral element that embodies the genuine community values of the Catholic tradition. Since the school is rightly considered an extension of the home, it ought to have "some of the amenities which can create a pleasant and family atmosphere."[63] This includes an adequate physical plant and adequate equipment.

It is especially important that this "school-home" be immediately recognizable as Catholic:

> From the first moment that a student sets foot in a Catholic school, he or she ought to have the impression of entering a new environment, one illumined by the light of faith, and having its own unique characteristics.[64]

The Incarnation, which emphasizes the *bodily* coming of God's Son into the world, leaves its seal on every aspect of Christian life. The very fact of the Incarnation tells us that the created world is the means God chose to communicate his life to us. What is human and visible can bear the divine.

If Catholic schools are to be true to their identity, they will suffuse their environment with a delight in the sacramental. Therefore they should express physically and visibly the external signs of Catholic culture through images, symbols, icons, and other objects of traditional devotion. A chapel, classroom crucifixes and statues, liturgical celebrations, and other sacramental reminders of Catholic life, including good art that is not explicitly religious in its subject matter, should be evident. All these signs embody the community ethos of Catholicism.

Prayer should be a normal part of the school day, so that students learn to pray in times of sorrow and joy, of disappointment and celebration, of difficulty and success. Such prayer teaches students that they belong to the communion of saints, a community that knows no bounds. The sacraments of the Eucharist and Reconciliation in particular should mark the rhythm of a Catholic school's life. Mass should be celebrated regularly, with the students and teachers participating appropriately. Traditional Catholic devotions should also have their place: praying the Rosary, decorating May altars, singing hymns, reading from the Bible, recounting the lives of the saints, and celebrating the Church's liturgical year. The sacramental vitality of the Catholic faith is expressed in these and similar acts of religion that belong to everyday ecclesial life and should be evident in every school.

4. IMBUED WITH A CATHOLIC WORLDVIEW THROUGHOUT ITS CURRICULUM

A fourth distinctive characteristic of Catholic schools is that the "spirit of Catholicism" should permeate the entire curriculum.

Catholic education is "intentionally directed to the growth of the whole person."[65] An integral education aims to develop gradually every capability of every student: his or her intellectual, physical, psychological, moral, and religious capacities. Vatican documents speak of an education that responds to all the needs of the human person:

> The integral formation of the human person, which is the purpose of education, includes the development of all the human faculties of the students, together with preparation for professional life, formation of ethical and social awareness, becoming aware of the transcendental, and religious education. Every

school, and every educator in the school, ought to be striving "to form strong and responsible individuals, who are capable of making free and correct choices," thus preparing young people "to open themselves more and more to reality, and to form in themselves a clear idea of the meaning of life" [*The Catholic School*, 31].[66]

To be integral or complete, Catholic schooling must be constantly inspired and guided by the gospel. As we have seen, the Catholic school would betray its purpose if it failed to found itself on the person of Christ and his teaching: "It derives all the energy necessary for its educational work from him."[67]

Because of the gospel's guiding role in a Catholic school, one might be tempted to think that the school's distinctiveness lies only in the quality of its religious instruction, catechesis, and pastoral activities. Nothing is further from the position of the Holy See. Rather, the Catholic school must embody its genuine catholicity even apart from such programs and projects. It is Catholic because it undertakes to educate the whole child, addressing the requirements of his or her natural and supernatural perfection. It is Catholic because it provides an education in the intellectual and moral virtues. It is Catholic because it prepares for a fully human life at the service of others and for the life of the world to come. All instruction, therefore, must be authentically Catholic in content and methodology across the entire program of studies.

Catholicism is a "comprehensive way of life"[68] that should animate every aspect of its activities and its curriculum. Although Vatican documents on education do not cover lesson planning, the order of teaching various subjects, or the relative merit of different pedagogical methods, the Holy See does provide guidelines meant to inspire the content of the curriculum. If a Catholic school is to deliver on its promise to provide students with an integral education, it must foster love for wisdom and truth, and must integrate faith, culture, and life.

Love for Wisdom and Passion for Truth

In an age of information overload, Catholic schools must be especially attentive in their instruction to strike the delicate balance between human experience and understanding. Catholic educators do not want their students to say, "We had the experience but missed the meaning."[69]

Knowledge and understanding are far more than the accumulation of information. T. S. Eliot puts it just right: "Where is the wisdom we have lost in knowledge? Where is the knowledge we have lost in information?"[70] Catholic schools do far more than convey information to passive students. They aspire to teach love for wisdom, habituating each student "to desire learning so much that he or she will delight in becoming a self-learner."[71]

Intrinsically related to the search for wisdom is another idea frequently repeated in Vatican teaching: the confidence that the human mind, however limited its powers, can come to a knowledge of truth. This conviction about the nature of truth is too important for Catholics to be confused about. Unlike skeptics and relativists, Catholic educators share a specific belief about truth: that, to a limited but real extent, it can be attained and communicated to others. Catholic schools take up the daunting task of freeing boys and girls from the insidious consequences of what Pope Benedict XVI has called the "dictatorship of relativism"[72] — a dictatorship that cripples all genuine education. Catholic teachers are to cultivate in themselves and develop in others a passion for truth that defeats moral and cultural relativism. They are to educate "in the truth."

Five Essential Marks of Catholic Schools

In an *ad limina* address to a group of American bishops, Pope John Paul II pinpointed the importance of having a correct grasp of truth if the Catholic Church's educational efforts are to bear fruit:

> The greatest challenge to Catholic education in the United States today, and the greatest contribution that authentically Catholic education can make to American culture, is to restore to that culture the conviction that human beings can grasp the truth of things, and, in grasping that truth, can know their duties to God, to themselves and their neighbors. . . . The contemporary world urgently needs the service of educational institutions that uphold and teach that truth is "that fundamental value without which freedom, justice, and human dignity are extinguished" [*Veritatis Splendor*, 4].[73]

Closely following papal teaching, the Holy See's documents on schools insist that education is about truth — in both its natural and its supernatural dimensions:

> The school considers human knowledge as a truth to be discovered. In the measure in which subjects are taught by someone who knowingly and without restraint seeks the truth, they are to that extent Christian. Discovery and awareness of truth leads man to the discovery of Truth itself.[74]

While Catholic schools conform to government-mandated curricula, they implement their programs with an overall religious orientation. Such a perspective includes criteria such as "confidence in our ability to attain truth, at least in a limited way — a confidence based not on feeling but on faith . . . [and] the ability to make judgments about what is true and what is false."[75] Unwavering commitment to truth is at home in an authentically Catholic school.

Faith, Culture, and Life

A second principle that derives from communicating a Catholic worldview to children is the notion that they should learn to transform culture in light of the gospel. Schools prepare students to relate the Catholic faith to their particular culture and to live that faith in practice.

In *The Catholic School on the Threshold of the Third Millennium*, the Congregation for Catholic Education commented:

> From the nature of the Catholic school also stems one of the most significant elements of its educational project: the synthesis between culture and faith. The endeavor to interweave reason and faith, which has become the heart of individual subjects, makes for

unity, articulation, and coordination, bringing forth within what is learned in a school a Christian vision of the world, of life, of culture, and of history.[76]

Schools form students within their own culture, teaching them an appreciation of its positive elements and fostering a more profound integration of the gospel in their particular situation. Faith and culture are intimately related, and students should be led, in ways suitable to the level of their intellectual development, to grasp the importance of this relationship. "We must always remember that, while faith is not to be identified with any one culture and is independent of all cultures, it must inspire every culture."[77]

Furthermore, young Catholics, in a way appropriate to their age, must also learn to make judgments based on religious and moral truths. They should learn to be critical and evaluative. It is the

Catholic faith that provides young people with the essential principles for critique and evaluation.[78]

The educational philosophy that guides Catholic schools also seeks to ensure that they are places where "faith, culture, and life are brought into harmony."[79] Central to the Catholic school is its mission of holiness, of saint-making. Mindful of redemption in Christ, the Catholic school aims to form in its pupils those particular virtues that will enable them to live a new life in Christ and help them to play their part in serving society and the Church. It strives to develop virtue "by the integration of culture with faith and of faith with living."[80] The Congregation for Catholic Education has written that "the Catholic school tries to create within its walls a climate in which the pupil's faith will gradually mature and enable him to assume the responsibility placed on him by Baptism."[81]

A primary way of helping Catholic students become more committed to their faith is by providing solid religious instruction. To be sure, "education in the faith is a part of the finality of a Catholic school."[82] For young Catholics, such instruction embraces both teaching the truths of the faith and fostering its practice.[83] Still, we must always take special care to avoid the error that a Catholic school's distinctiveness rests solely on the shoulders of its religious-education program. Such a position would foster the misunderstanding that faith and life can be divorced, that religion is a merely private affair without doctrinal content or moral obligations.

5. SUSTAINED BY GOSPEL WITNESS

A final indicator of a school's authentic catholicity is the vital witness of its teachers and administrators. With them lies the primary responsibility for creating a Christian school climate, as individuals and as a community.[84] Indeed, "it depends chiefly on them whether the Catholic school achieves its purpose."[85] Consequently the Holy See's documents pay a great deal of attention to the vocation of teachers and their participation in the Church's evangelizing mission. Theirs is a supernatural calling and not simply the exercise of a profession.[86] "The nobility of the task to which teachers are called demands that, in imitation of Christ, the only Teacher, they reveal the Christian message not only by word but also by every gesture of their behavior."[87]

More than a master who teaches, a Catholic educator is a person who gives testimony by his or her life. Shortly after his election, Pope Benedict XVI spoke about the kind of witness required of all teachers of the faith, including those in Catholic schools:

> The central figure in the work of educating . . . is specifically the form of witness. . . . The witness never refers to himself but to something, or rather, to Someone greater than he, whom he has encountered and whose dependable goodness he has sampled. Thus, every educator and witness finds an unequaled model in Jesus Christ, the Father's great witness, who said nothing about himself but spoke as the Father had taught him [cf. John 8:28].[88]

Hiring Committed Catholics

To fulfill their responsibility of speaking about the Father, educators in Catholic schools, with very few exceptions, should be practicing Catholics who are committed to the Church and living her sacramental life. Despite the difficulties sometimes involved, those responsible for hiring teachers must see to it that these criteria are met. When addressing Catholic-school principals in the *National Directory for Catechesis* (2005), the American bishops give unequivocal direction: "Recruit teachers who are practicing Catholics, who can understand and accept the teachings of the Catholic Church and the moral demands of the gospel, and who can contribute to the achievement of the school's Catholic identity and apostolic goals."[89] Elsewhere the bishops also affirmed, "While some situations might entail compelling reasons for members of another faith tradition to teach in a Catholic school, as much as possible, all teachers in a Catholic school should be practicing Catholics."[90]

When such a policy is ignored, it is inevitable that children will absorb, even if they are not explicitly taught, a soft indifferentism that will sustain neither their practice of the faith nor their ability to imbue society with Christian values. Principals, pastors, school-board members, parents, and bishops share in the serious duty of hiring teachers who meet the standards of doctrine and integrity of life essential to a flourishing Catholic school.

The Holy See shares the solicitude of the American bishops about employing teachers with a clear understanding of and commitment to Catholic education. A primary way to foster a school's catholicity is by carefully hiring men and women who enthusiastically endorse its distinctive ethos, for Catholic education is strengthened by witnesses to the gospel.

Transparent Witness of Life

As well as fostering a Catholic worldview across the curriculum, even in so-called secular subjects, "if students in Catholic schools are to gain a genuine experience of the Church, the example of teachers and others responsible for their formation is crucial: the witness of adults in the school community is a vital part of the school's identity."[91]

Children will pick up far more by the example of their educators than by masterful pedagogical techniques, especially in the practice of Christian virtues. In the words of Pope Benedict XVI:

> The central figure in the work of educating, and especially in education in the faith, which is the summit of the person's formation and is his or her most appropriate horizon, is specifically the form of witness. This witness becomes a proper reference point to the extent that the person can account for the hope that nourishes his life [cf. 1 Pet. 3:15] and is personally involved in the truth that he proposes.[92]

The prophetic words of Pope Paul VI ring as true today as they did more than thirty years ago:

"Modern man listens more willingly to witnesses than to teachers, and if he does listen to teachers, it is because they are witnesses."[93] What educators do and how they act are more significant than what they say — inside and outside the classroom. This is how the Church evangelizes. "The more completely an educator can give concrete witness to the model of the ideal person [Christ] that is being presented to the students, the more this ideal will be believed and imitated."[94]

Hypocrisy turns off today's students. While their demands are high, perhaps sometimes even unreasonably so, if teachers fail to model fidelity to the truth and virtuous behavior, then even the best of curricula cannot successfully embody a Catholic school's distinctive ethos. For example, if teachers and administrators demonstrate the individualistic and competitive ethic that now marks so much public education, they will fail to inspire students with the values of solidarity and community, even if they praise those values verbally. The same can be said about a failure to give clear witness to the Church's teaching on the sanctity of marriage and the inviolability of human life.

Catholic educators are expected to be models for their students by bearing transparent witness to Christ and to the beauty of the gospel. If boys and girls are to experience the splendor of the Church, the Christian example of teachers and others responsible for their formation is indispensable, and no effort should be spared in guaranteeing the presence of such witness in every Catholic school.

Conclusion

The Holy See, through papal interventions and the documents of the Congregation for Catholic Education, recognizes the priceless treasure of Catholic schools as an indispensable instrument of evangelization. Ensuring their genuinely Catholic identity is the Church's greatest educational challenge.

Complementing the primary role of parents in educating their children, such schools, which should be accessible, affordable, and available to all, build up the community of believers, evangelize the culture, and serve the common good of society.

I would like to conclude this essay with a suggestion that might help to strengthen the Catholic identity of America's elementary and secondary schools. In the United States, various accrediting agencies monitor the institutional effectiveness of schools' educational activities. They look at outcomes that can be measured, using a wide variety of means, and ask the schools to show that they use the results of their assessment to improve their mission effectiveness. Quite simply, accreditors ask: *How do you know that you are achieving what you say you are? What steps are you taking to improve your effectiveness?*

Should not Catholic schools, precisely insofar as they claim to be specified by their catholicity, do something along the same lines? They too could engage in quality assurance — that is, assurance of their Catholic identity. How does a Catholic school know whether it is achieving its specific mission? What steps is it taking to foster its catholicity? Such a "Catholic" accreditation process would involve an internal review of the five benchmark indicators — as well as others that could be developed. Teachers, administrators, bishops, parents,

Conclusion

and school-board members would all take part in the review. This collaborative and systematic exercise of assessing a school's catholicity would serve to identify, clarify, and strengthen its effectiveness in its service of Christ and the Church.

✛ *J. Michael Miller, CSB*
Secretary
Congregation for Catholic Education

Notes

1 United States Conference of Catholic Bishops (USCCB), *Renewing Our Commitment to Catholic Elementary and Secondary Schools in the Third Millennium* (Washington, DC: United States Conference of Catholic Bishops, 2005), introduction.

2 Second Vatican Ecumenical Council, *Gravissimum Educationis*, introduction; cf. *Code of Canon Law*, canon 794 § 1.

3 Congregation for Catholic Education, *The Catholic School on the Threshold of the Third Millennium*, 11; cf. Sacred Congregation for Catholic Education, *The Catholic School*, 9; Congregation for Catholic Education, *The*

Religious Dimension of Education in a Catholic School, 33.

4   Cf. *The Religious Dimension of Education in a Catholic School*, 44.

5   Cf. *Renewing Our Commitment to Catholic Elementary and Secondary Schools in the Third Millennium*, 5.

6   Kenneth C. Jones, *Index of Leading Catholic Indicators: The Church Since Vatican II* (St. Louis: Oriens Publishing Company, 2003), 36.

7   Cf. *Idem*.

8   John Paul II, *Vita Consecrata*, 96; cf. Congregation for Catholic Education, *Consecrated Persons and Their Mission in Schools: Reflections and Guidelines*, 29.

9   Sacred Congregation for Catholic Education, *Lay Catholics in Schools: Witnesses to Faith*, 37.

[10] *Ibid.*, 60.

[11] Second Vatican Ecumenical Council, *Apostolicam Actuositatem*, 25.

[12] Cf. *Gravissimum Educationis*, 3, 6; John Paul II, *Familiaris Consortio*, 36; *Lay Catholics in Schools*, 12; Pontifical Council for the Family, *Charter of the Rights of the Family* (22 October 1983), 1-3; *Code of Canon Law*, canon 793; *Catechism of the Catholic Church*, n. 2229; John Paul II, *Letter to Families*, 16; Pontifical Council for Justice and Peace, *Compendium of the Social Doctrine of the Church* (Vatican City: Vatican Press, 2005), n. 239.

[13] Peter Redpath, foreword in Curtis L. Hancock, *Recovering a Catholic Philosophy of Elementary Education* (Mount Pocono, Pennsylvania: Newman House Press, 2005), 19.

[14] Cf. *Code of Canon Law*, canon 796; *The Catholic School*, 8.

[15] John Paul II, *Letter to Families*, 16; cf. Benedict XVI, Angelus Address (28 October 2005): *L'Osservatore Romano*, English-language edition (2 November 2005), 1: "Parents are the primary and principal educators and are assisted by civil society in accordance with the principle of subsidiarity (cf. *Gravissimum Educationis*, 3)."

[16] *Lay Catholics in Schools*, 14; cf. *The Catholic School on the Threshold of the Third Millennium*, 16.

[17] *The Catholic School*, 13.

[18] *Gravissimum Educationis*, 6; cf. *Code of Canon Law*, canon 793 § 2.

19 *Compendium of Social Doctrine of the Church*, n. 241.

20 Cf. *Code of Canon Law*, canon 797; Jason Boffetti, *All Schools Are Public Schools: A Case for State Aid to Private Education and Homeschooling Parents* (Washington, DC: Faith and Reason Institute, 2001).

21 Cf. *Renewing Our Commitment to Catholic Elementary and Secondary Schools in the Third Millennium*, 12.

22 *Gravissimum Educationis*, 9; cf. *Consecrated Persons and Their Mission in Schools*, 69-72.

23 *The Catholic School on the Threshold of the Third Millennium*, 15; *The Catholic School*, 58; *Consecrated Persons and Their Mission in Schools*, 70: "Sometimes, however, it is Catholic educational institutions themselves that have strayed from such a preferential

option [for the poor], which characterized the beginnings of the majority of institutes of consecrated life devoted to teaching."

24 John Paul II, *Ad Limina* Address to American Bishops of the Ecclesiastical Provinces of Portland in Oregon, Seattle, and Anchorage (24 June 2004), 1: *Origins*, 34:14 (16 September 2004), 220-221.

25 Cf. *The Catholic School on the Threshold of the Third Millennium*, 11.

26 Michael J. Guerra, "Catholic Schools in the United States: A Gift to the Church and a Gift to the Nation," *Seminarium*, 1/2 (2004), 105.

27 Cf. *The Catholic School*, 29.

28 Cf. *Gravissimum Educationis*, 8.

29 John Paul II, Address to Catholic Educators
    (12 September 1987), 7: *Origins*, 17:15
    (1 October 1987), 270.

30 Cf. Hancock, *Recovering a Catholic
    Philosophy of Education*, 34.

31 *Lay Catholics in Schools*, 18; cf. *The Religious
    Dimension of Education in a Catholic School*,
    63; *Consecrated Persons and Their Mission in
    Schools*, 35.

32 Second Vatican Ecumenical Council,
    Gaudium et Spes, 22; cf. *The Catholic
    School on the Threshold of the Third
    Millennium*, 9.

33 *The Catholic School on the Threshold of
    the Third Millennium*, 9; cf. *Lay Catholics
    in Schools*, 18.

34 *The Catholic School*, 35.

35 John Paul II, Message to the National Catholic Educational Association of the United States (16 April 1979) *Insegnamenti*, 2 (1979): 919-920.

36 *The Catholic School*, 34.

37 *The Religious Dimension of Education in a Catholic School*, 25.

38 *Lay Catholics in Schools*, 41.

39 John Paul II, *Novo Millennio Ineunte*, 43.

40 *Lay Catholics in Schools*, 22.

41 *The Religious Dimension of Education in a Catholic School*, 31; cf. *The Catholic School on the Threshold of the Third Millennium*, 18.

42 *The Religious Dimension of Education in a Catholic School*, 40.

43 Cf. *Lay Catholics in Schools*, 78.

44 Cf. *Consecrated Persons and Their Mission in Schools*, 16.

45 *Ibid.*, 46.

46 *The Religious Dimension of Education in a Catholic School*, 42: cf. *Lay Catholics in Schools*, 34.

47 *Consecrated Persons and Their Mission in Schools*, 17; cf. 41.

48 *Ibid.*, 46.

49 Cf. John Paul II, *Novo Millennio Ineunte*, 43.

50 John Paul II, *Ad Limina* Address to American Bishops (28 October 1983), 7: *Insegnamenti*, 6/2 (1983), 891.

51 Cf. *Code of Canon Law*, canon 375.

52 Canon 794.

[53] John Paul II, *Pastores Gregis*, 52.

[54] Cf. *Code of Canon Law*, canon 806 § 1; cf. *Consecrated Persons and Their Mission in Schools*, 42.

[55] Cf. *Code of Canon Law*, canon 803 § 2.

[56] John Paul II, *Ad Limina* Address to American Bishops of the Ecclesiastical Provinces of Portland in Oregon, Seattle, and Anchorage (24 June 2004), 3: *Origins*, 34:14 (16 September 2004), 221.

[57] Cf. John Paul II, *Pastores Gregis*, 51.

[58] Cf. *Consecrated Persons and Their Mission in Schools*, 61.

[59] Cited in *Consecrated Persons and Their Mission in Schools*, 62.

[60] *The Catholic School on the Threshold of the Third Millennium*, 18.

[61] *Lay Catholics in Schools*, 33.

[62] *Consecrated Persons and Their Mission in Schools*, 62.

[63] *The Religious Dimension of Education in a Catholic School*, 27.

[64] *Ibid.*, 25.

[65] *Ibid.*, 29.

[66] Lay Catholics in Schools, 17; cf. *The Religious Dimension of Education in a Catholic School*, 99.

[67] *The Catholic School*, 55.

[68] R. Scott Appleby, "Catholicism as a Comprehensive Way of Life," *Origins*, 32:22 (7 November 2002), 370.

[69] "Dry Salvages."

[70] "Choruses from 'The Rock' 1934."

[71] Hancock, *Recovering a Catholic Philosophy of Elementary Education*, 77.

[72] Joseph Ratzinger, Homily for Mass *Pro Eligendo Romano Pontific* (18 April 2005): *Origins*, 34:45 (28 April 2005), 720.

[73] John Paul II, *Ad Limina* Address to Bishops from Illinois, Indiana, and Wisconsin (30 May 1998), 3: *Origins*, 28:5 (18 June 1998), 76.

[74] *The Catholic School*, 41.

[75] *The Religious Dimension of Education in a Catholic School*, 57.

[76] Cf. *The Catholic School on the Threshold of the Third Millennium*, 14.

77 *The Religious Dimension of Education in a Catholic School*, 53.

78 *Lay Catholics in Schools*, 20.

79 *The Religious Dimension of Education of a Catholic School*, 34; cf. *The Catholic School*, 44.

80 *The Catholic School*, 49; cf. 36.

81 *The Catholic School*, 47; cf. *Gravissimum Educationis*, 8.

82 *Lay Catholics in Schools*, 43.

83 Cf. *The Catholic School*, 50-51; *The Religious Dimension of Education in a Catholic School*, 66-69.

84 Cf. *The Religious Dimension of Education in a Catholic School*, 26; *The Catholic School on the Threshold of the Third Millennium*, 19.

[85] *Gravissimum Educationis*, 8.

[86] Cf. *Lay Catholics in Schools*, 37; cf.
*The Catholic School on the Threshold
of the Third Millennium*, 19.

[87] *The Catholic School*, 43.

[88] Benedict XVI, Address to the Participants
in the Ecclesial Diocesan Convention of Rome
(6 June 2005): *L'Osservatore Romano*, English-language edition (15 June 2005), 7.

[89] United States Conference of Catholic
Bishops, *National Directory for Catechesis*
(Washington, DC: United States Confer-
ence of Catholic Bishops, 2005), 231.

[90] *Ibid.*, 233.

[91] John Paul II, *Ad Limina* Address to
Bishops from Illinois, Indiana, and
Wisconsin (30 May 1998), 4: *Origins,*

28:5 (18 June 1998), 77; cf. *Lay Catholics in Schools*, 32, 40.

[92] Benedict XVI, Address to the Participants in the Ecclesial Diocesan Convention of Rome (6 June 2005): *L'Osservatore Romano*, English-language edition (15 June 2005), 7.

[93] Paul VI, *Evangelii Nuntiandi*, 41.

[94] *Lay Catholics in Schools*, 32.

The Solidarity Association

The Solidarity Association is founded in love for
Jesus Christ and His Church. We believe that in a
"solidarity with all men, living or dead, which is
founded on the communion of saints, the least of
our acts done in charity redounds to the profit of all"
(*Catechism of the Catholic Church*, n. 953).

We embrace the truths and challenges to the
laity expressed in the documents of Vatican Council II and, in particular, in *Apostolicam Actuositatem*
(Decree on the Apostolate of the Laity), wherein
we are called to "engage in the apostolate through
the faith, hope, and charity which the Holy Spirit
diffuses in the hearts of all members of the Church.
Indeed, by the precept of charity, which is the Lord's
greatest commandment, all the faithful are impelled

to promote the glory of God through the coming of His kingdom and to obtain eternal life for all men — that they may know the only true God and Him whom He sent, Jesus Christ [cf. John 17:3]. On all Christians therefore is laid the preeminent responsibility of working to make the divine message of salvation known and accepted by all men throughout the world." We have also drawn inspiration from the wisdom set forth in *Christifideles Laici* (On the Vocation and the Mission of the Lay Faithful in the Church and in the World).

The association is a canonically approved Private Association of the Christian Faithful with juridical personality. We are faithful and obedient to the Holy Father and embrace and beseech the help and protection of the Blessed Virgin Mary.